FROM MY ROSY LIPS
By Princess Yvonne Dumas
*A nod to Haiku**

Cover photo: Prin's rosy lips
Printed in the United States of America

Introduction

I love poetry. There are so many styles: rhyming, sonnets, epic, and many more. One of my favorite poetry tools hails from Japan in the form of Haiku.

Haiku poetry tends to use nature for imagery and metaphor, but it follows a very specific format of 3 lines. The first line has 5 syllables, the second has 7 syllables, and the last line has 5 syllables again. The topics of the poems can range to be about anything – love, happiness, sadness, the routines of life – anything goes.

For this book, I chose mostly to capture some aspect of nature or life in a metaphor or simile, and I explore the topic of love the most. Is this romantic love poetry? Maybe. I'm not sure I should say. I think that's the really amazing thing about Haiku style – it's so short that it puts the interpretation in the hands of the reader. I know what I meant, but do you? That's the beauty of this poetry tool.

Enjoy!

How to Use This Book

This book is a poetry book and a poetry prompt journal! We will be focusing on the Haiku style and creating space for you to put on your own creative cap to make a Haiku of your own. You'll do this by pulling from my work to recreate your own original ideas.

How do you do this?

Read my Haiku. You can choose to do each of the interactive parts after reading each poem, or you can read all of the Haiku entries first. Then, do the interactive portion.

The following is a sample of the interactive page and how to use it.

Instructions: (This will be the page after each Haiku.)
Using my Haiku, write a word from the poem that stands out to you or feels important to the poem. In the next 2 columns, write a synonym or related word, an alternate you could use to say something similar. Repeat this process until you have a few words and alternate expressions. At the bottom, create your own 5 syllable, 7 syllable, and 5 syllable Haiku!

Prin's Haiku Words	My Alternate Idea	My Alternate Idea
Ice	Snow	Cold
Frost	Freezing	Sleet
Beloved	Darling	Adored
Love	Devotion	Intimacy

My Original Haiku

5 The snow is falling
7 Freezing my bones and heart -
5 My devotion gone.

Let's begin...

The ice has melted.
My beloved frost is gone...
The heart can love now.

Your Turn

Instructions:
Using my Haiku, write a word from the poem that stands out to you or feels important to the poem. In the next 2 columns, write a synonym or related word, an alternate you could use to say something similar. Repeat this process until you have a few words and alternate expressions. At the bottom, create your own 5 syllable, 7 syllable, and 5 syllable Haiku!

Prin's Haiku Words	My Alternate Idea	My Alternate Idea

My Original Haiku

5	
7	
5	

A rabbit hole mouth,
Full of promises and soul -
I drink from his lips.

Your Turn

Prin's Haiku Words	My Alternate Idea	My Alternate Idea

My Original Haiku

5
7
5

**Cloud cotton up there,
My fingers graze the warm air –
Pareidolia.**

Your Turn

Prin's Haiku Words	My Alternate Idea	My Alternate Idea

My Original Haiku

5
7
5

I searched for the sun
In eyes made of deep blue flames -
My world scorched by fire.

Your Turn

Prin's Haiku Words	My Alternate Idea	My Alternate Idea

My Original Haiku

5
7
5

**Ballads play by winds,
The marching of winter waves,
Always in fine tune.**

Your Turn

Prin's Haiku Words	My Alternate Idea	My Alternate Idea

My Original Haiku

5
7
5

My love belongs here,
Inside a still dark cavern -
Forever in peace.

Your Turn

Prin's Haiku Words	My Alternate Idea	My Alternate Idea

My Original Haiku

5
7
5

I kill you quickly,
Compassion from the tiger -
Survival of prey.

Your Turn

Prin's Haiku Words	My Alternate Idea	My Alternate Idea

My Original Haiku

5
7
5

He spoke in riddles;
I sit by the tree with ax...
Teach him math angles.

Your Turn

Prin's Haiku Words	My Alternate Idea	My Alternate Idea

My Original Haiku

5
7
5

**In a cat cradle,
I hid a great home - one day -
Until I woke up.**

Your Turn

Prin's Haiku Words	My Alternate Idea	My Alternate Idea

My Original Haiku

5	
7	
5	

Butterfly can't fly
With nasty winds full of hairs
That fell out of her.

Your Turn

Prin's Haiku Words	My Alternate Idea	My Alternate Idea

My Original Haiku

5
7
5

This star came by me
Following me everywhere,
Killing my shadows.

Your Turn

Prin's Haiku Words	My Alternate Idea	My Alternate Idea

My Original Haiku

5
7
5

I wanted this child,
But he did not want old me...
Oh, he chose the sea.

Your Turn

Prin's Haiku Words	My Alternate Idea	My Alternate Idea

My Original Haiku

5	
7	
5	

The laughter inside
This little bright hermit shell
I tossed up today.

Your Turn

Prin's Haiku Words	My Alternate Idea	My Alternate Idea

My Original Haiku

5
7
5

I crave nights of rage
Heat keeps all of me dripping -
I've made him my mop.

Your Turn

Prin's Haiku Words	My Alternate Idea	My Alternate Idea

My Original Haiku

5
7
5

The moon followed me.
I ran until I stopped – crash!
Hit oblivion.

Your Turn

Prin's Haiku Words	My Alternate Idea	My Alternate Idea

My Original Haiku

5	
7	
5	

You'll think of roses,
You'll get lost in fantasies,
But never know me.

Your Turn

Prin's Haiku Words	My Alternate Idea	My Alternate Idea

My Original Haiku

5
7
5

Duckling scared in flight,
Motors off in the distance –
Desperate hero.

Your Turn

Prin's Haiku Words	My Alternate Idea	My Alternate Idea

My Original Haiku

5
7
5

**Magnanimous lake,
Letting me live through the frost –
Stubborn feet won't leave.**

Your Turn

Prin's Haiku Words	My Alternate Idea	My Alternate Idea

My Original Haiku

5	
7	
5	

**Blueberries burst blue,
Juices flow everywhere now –
Tongue feels like summer.**

Your Turn

Prin's Haiku Words	My Alternate Idea	My Alternate Idea

My Original Haiku

5
7
5

I lusted for grapes,
Wanting them rolled on my skin –
Alas, I crave milk.

Your Turn

Prin's Haiku Words	My Alternate Idea	My Alternate Idea

My Original Haiku

5
7
5

Falling leaves whither.
The sturdy tree has gone bald.
Winter killed autumn.

Your Turn

Prin's Haiku Words	My Alternate Idea	My Alternate Idea

My Original Haiku

5
7
5

I climb the mountain,
Out of air, lacking the strength...
Arms flail – precipice.

Your Turn

Prin's Haiku Words	My Alternate Idea	My Alternate Idea

My Original Haiku

5
7
5

Horse wild through meadows,
Hoof prints on gloomy petals –
My bouquet is gone.

Your Turn

Prin's Haiku Words	My Alternate Idea	My Alternate Idea

My Original Haiku

5
7
5

A fire within flesh,
The smell of sulfur and balm –
Passionate heart beats.

Your Turn

Prin's Haiku Words	My Alternate Idea	My Alternate Idea

My Original Haiku

5
7
5

Thirst, a distraction.
No water, welcome respite.
Numb me from the loss.

Your Turn

Prin's Haiku Words	My Alternate Idea	My Alternate Idea

My Original Haiku

5
7
5

She woke up too late.
Fake lips stealing ideas –
Eats insects for art.

Your Turn

Prin's Haiku Words	My Alternate Idea	My Alternate Idea

My Original Haiku

5
7
5

I make it easy,
Love to inhale the sunlight –
Sparkle from inside.

Your Turn

Prin's Haiku Words	My Alternate Idea	My Alternate Idea

My Original Haiku

5
7
5

I bear fruit and smile,
A seedless weed will not know –
I know the secret.

Your Turn

Prin's Haiku Words	My Alternate Idea	My Alternate Idea

My Original Haiku

5
7
5

Salt and sand in hand,
Clenching fists of old mountains –
A day at the beach.

Your Turn

Prin's Haiku Words	My Alternate Idea	My Alternate Idea

My Original Haiku

5
7
5

I love like rivers.
Ephemeral or quite old –
Stay or leave my stream.

Your Turn

Prin's Haiku Words	My Alternate Idea	My Alternate Idea

My Original Haiku

5
7
5

Moonlight tricked us both.
We lay on grass by midnight –
Ears pressed to Earth's core.

Your Turn

Prin's Haiku Words	My Alternate Idea	My Alternate Idea

My Original Haiku

5	
7	
5	

Scent of spring's flowers,
And ah, how I breathe it in –
Memories of you.

Your Turn

Prin's Haiku Words	My Alternate Idea	My Alternate Idea

My Original Haiku

5
7
5

**Turtles turned over,
And one knows the way to leave –
Walk away slowly.**

Your Turn

Prin's Haiku Words	My Alternate Idea	My Alternate Idea

My Original Haiku

5
7
5

**Potent poison sting,
Hands in torment – a tattoo –
A scorpion kiss.**

Your Turn

Prin's Haiku Words	My Alternate Idea	My Alternate Idea

My Original Haiku

5	
7	
5	

When the air changes,
I am forever free here –
A bird talks to mites.

Your Turn

Prin's Haiku Words	My Alternate Idea	My Alternate Idea

My Original Haiku

5
7
5

**Soothing lull of trees,
Tousled in the distance – Stop!
Not all flames comfort.**

Your Turn

Prin's Haiku Words	My Alternate Idea	My Alternate Idea

My Original Haiku

5
7
5

*Do you see it now -
The title page of this book?
It is a Haiku. ☺

Thank you for sharing this space with me to create and enjoy sharing our creations together.

I hope you were able to spend some calming moments developing ideas for your own Haiku poems.

A few things to note before I leave:

Haiku does not have to be capitalized like a proper noun, but I did so out of respect to the poem style and its cultural origin. Growing up, my father traveled often to Japan, China, and other countries in Asia, and many elements of those cultures were an inherent part of my home even though I have no personal ethnic claim to them. Thank you to the Japanese people for sharing such a wonderful way to express poetic thoughts in a brief and mindful manner many centuries ago.

On another note, this wraps up the third book I published in 2021, after the "fun" of creating at home during pandemic lockdowns. I have a few more book ideas up my sleeve, but I hope this one becomes a part of your creative journey. During stressful times, the most effective forms of healing come from within you.

Thank you,
Prin

For more information about my writing and upcoming projects, check out www.writingbyprin.com. You can also check out my music at www.musicbyprin.com or follow my website community for my last book, The C.A.L.M. PRINciples at www.thecalmprinciples.com.

Make it a great life!
I always say to Love big!
Do the thing – like stars!

www.ingramcontent.com/pod-product-compliance
Lightning Source LLC
Chambersburg PA
CBHW031409160726
47993CB00003B/1151